Love Poems

For

That Fine Girl!

Barry Thomas's

Love PoeMs For That Fine Girl!

This book I dedicate to: "My Beautiful Black Sisters"
Who along with our Heavenly Father,
Made me and the following pages possible.

My Beautiful Black Sisters

Oh! You All are the Spice of Life!
Without You; There would never be the possibility of Me.
Every Man can walk around with His chest out;
But He plus any other being;
Could have never produced anything, Without
My Beautiful Black Sisters!
People in the media, can talk about The Black
Broken Family, All Day Long; But from Big Mama Nem,
To the Young Sisters in the Hood Today!
They have Always been the Ones, Who Gave Us True Love.
Let Me tell Y'all Sisters something: You All are A Wonder!
In The Beginning; The Creator Revealed to The Universe,
That: My Beautiful Black Sisters
Are The Key To Life!
You were the First Ones
To Raise the Children in The Village.
You Were The First Teachers.
You All are Better than any Religion made by Man.
It was You, who introduced Us to Our Heavenly Father!
Through Him, you showed us how to Live a Holy Life.
Just to be in Your Presence; Makes My Body Quiver,
And tears are flowing from My Face,
While writing the rough draft of this poem.
When the Light Shines on You;
My Beautiful Black Sisters;
Even Your Shadow has A Glow!
If All of You would disappear from the Planet Today,
All Life form left behind;
Wouldn't last a second without You.
My Beautiful Black Sisters!

I Love Y'all Much Too Much!
If Anything Bad would Ever happen to You;
I Don't Think I could Live.
I Don't know what in the World I Would Do.
Some may say, I'm using these Words as a Clutch;
But, That's Not it at All.
I Love Y'all Much Too Much!

Since We All First Met;
This has Been the Best Ride, I have Ever Had!
I Wanna Thank Y'all and I Will Never Let Y'all Down.
There is Nothing Y'all Can Ever Do;
That Could Ever Make Me Sad.

When We All Come Together;
Every Moment is So Much Fun!
I Look Forward Every Day to Waking Up to
God, you and the morning sun.

I Love The Way Y'all Release Your Love On Me!
You All are So Smart, So Sexy and So Dynamic and
Y'all have the Most Beautiful and Gentle Touch.
These are Some of the Reasons; Why:
I Love Y'all Much Too Much!

My Beautiful Black Sisters,
You All are A Blessing and You All have
Brought Me A Whole Lot of Luck!
This is The Main Reason, Why:
I Love Y'all Much Too Much!

Contents

Contents

Contents

TUSKEGEE UNIVERSITY
Commencement
August 1, 1986

Look Mama, We Did It!

For You

Girl, For You
I Will Do Most Anything.
I know that compared to God,
I have a small mind.
But, I'm Being Honest, When I say:
If I was with Him in the Beginning,
When He was Creating
The Heavens and The Worlds;
And After Being in the Middle of It;
Every other Minute,
I would keep reminding you, That:
"You are the Original Girl"
Whether Our Creator was Starting from
The Beginning or Finishing the Ending!
No Matter, How Deep or How Far,
I Would Stop Every Thing!
Just to go and get You,
Your favorite candy bar!
I know to some, This may sound irrational,
Or It may not sound sane.
But to Prove My Love; For You Girl,
At This Given Moment,
I will go outside and stand in the rain;
And won't return, until
The Membership in the PGA is Over 99% Black!
Then The World Will No longer be Surprise!
When Someone with Tiger's Ability and Skin Tone,
Can Master the game and yet still Win,
With So Much Slack!

That Fine Girl!

Girl, You are So Fine;
That I can Look at You;
Through the Sun-Rays;
And Tell the Time!
I'm Telling A Truth,
So, You know I'm not Lying.
Girl, You are So Fine!
When I See Your Figure;
Look Love:
The Blood Rushes,
All Over My Body And Makes
My Heart and other Organs Grow Bigger!
Girl, You are So Fine;
That the sell of Gold; Has not reach its peak.
With That Body: You can make the
Mummies In Egypt Speak!
Girl, I Love Seeing Your Beautiful Smile!
Did You Know?
That the bees and mosquitoes,
That they said was the queen and left the Nile;
Were trying to find You;
To View Your Beauty and Style;
Up Close and Personal,
By Traveling Thousands of Miles!
I just wanted to introduce You,
To the World!
Cause, You Will Always Be:
That Fine Girl!

Your Big Brown Eyes

Girl, When I See,
Your Big Brown Eyes,
They remind me of
The Queen of the Nile.
Your Big Brown Eyes
Are So Pretty;
Every Time I See Them,
I Just Can't Stop Acting Silly.
Woman, You Will Always Be My Girl;
And We Are Going to Show,
Your Big Brown Eyes,
To The Whole Wide World.
My Beautiful Black Sister,
Your Big Brown Eyes
Are So Beautiful!
And You Know,
I Always Tell You That!
So, You Know,
I'm not playing any Antics.
Your Big Brown Eyes,
Can Realign,
All of The Distance Planets...!
I Am So Happy,
That You Are
My Girlfriend!
Therefore; I Know
I Will Continue To See:
Your Big Brown Eyes,
Again and Again!

Slow And Easy Love

Have you ever been with a Girl and
You knew from the start, that it would be a
Slow And Easy Love?
That's the Situation,
I'm Experiencing with
That Fine Girl!
She is the Most Beautiful Person
In The Whole Entire World.
That's why it's Worth the wait, to pursue this
Slow And Easy Love.
This Sister is So Badd!
Every Time She Walks on the Streets:
Every Man Takes a Double Take;
Looks Again; Then Repeat and Repeat;
Before, taking back his original seat!
She is not an Ordinary Girl!
That's the reason why,
I will never give up on this,
Slow And Easy Love.
You can Line Up, All of the So Call
Beautiful Hollywood Stars, From Wall to Wall;
With my pick, I'm Choosing
That Fine Girl!
Without A Pause!
It does not matter how long it takes
For Me to get into Her World; Because,
I'm Going to Enjoy Making with Her,
What We Call:
Slow And Easy Love!

An Ole Fashion Girl

I'm in Love with
An Ole Fashion Girl.
If you could ever meet Her;
You too would write
Poems and Songs about Her World.
I have Never Seen Any One
With So Much Style and Grace.
If All of the People on the Planet,
Would vanish today;
I truly believe that our Creator,
Could use This Fine Sister,
As the Primary Vessel to
Re-Populate The Entire Human Race.
This Beautiful Black Sister,
Gives So Much Love,
To Every One that She comes in contact with.
I Tell You No Lie;
Every Time, I See this Woman;
My Spirit, My Soul and My Body,
Gets an Electric Lift.
This Beauty is So Down to Earth!
For Her, I'll Tackle The Roughest Waters
And Ride on a Board and Surf.
I'm Willing and Able to give this Sister,
All of the Diamonds, Pearls and
Fine Gems in the World.
Cause, Without Her,
There Would Never Be:
An Ole Fashion Girl!

So, Call Me Up!

Girl, You know I don't pretend.
I want to make You All Mine.
I'm not One who Falls in Love with a Woman;
Then waste Her Time.
I want to Hold You Close and
I Will Never Turn You Away.
If need be, I'll Stay Home All Day.
So, Call Me Up!
I Guarantee You; I will answer the phone.
That's why I'm pleading: Baby, Come Turn Me On.
Once We Show Our True Love,
Within Our Relationship.
There Will Never be Any Doubt, that what We Have,
Has Been Spiritual Built!
Baby, You can be My Lover,
My Friend and My Main Squeeze;
But after Months of Flirting;
Please! Don't be just a tease.
Girl, I want to Make You All Mine and
That's for Sure.
But, There's so much that My Heart can Endure.
So, Call Me Up!
I Guarantee You, I'll answer the phone.
There's So Much Love, Inside of Me and You.
Therefore: You know What to Do!
Baby, Come Turn Me On!
I'll be waiting for You at Home; Because,
There's no time to Pass the Buck;
So, Baby Please, Call Me Up!

I Can't Get That Sister
Off of My Mind!

They say that it takes time to make good wine;
But I can't waste any of my time, Because:
I Can't Get That Sister Off of My Mind!

I have never seen Anyone Like Her before.
She is So Fine and Graceful;
That when She Walks,
The Worlds Clocks:
"Tick More than they Tock"
And their second hand,
Every other minute;
Fails and misses the Mark.

Her Face is Gorgeous and So Pretty;
That when I'm in Her Presence, I'm the One,
Who Feels Good and Gets All Giddy.

I'm about to have a Serious Talk with that Nurse.
Because, my Emotions are So High!
I'm the One About to Bust!

I'll let Y'all in on a little secret:
At this particular moment
I really don't care about the time.
Cause;
I'm So Glad That:
I Can't Get That Sister Off of My Mind!

I Want To Make My Love
A Part of You

I Got So Much Love to Give and It's All for You.
I Want To Make My Love A Part of You!
For All of the Obstacles that have come Our way;
And All of the things that People might say.
At this moment, this is a Brand New Day.
Look at where We are in the short span,
That We have known One Another, and
Where We are projected to be in Record Time.
I Want To Make My Love A Part of You!
Mainly for Spiritual Reasons and of Course;
It Doesn't Hurt that You are So Doggone Fine!
I know We are in a Situation,
Where There's Not An Easy Way Out;
I Got So Much Love to Give and
My Love is Gonna Get Ya in Areas,
Which have never been Sought!
I Love Being in your Presence: Twenty-Four/Seven!
It's not Hard to Explain: It Just Feels Like Heaven!
People tease me about it, All the time, It doesn't matter;
I don't care what They say or do. Because:
I Want To Make My Love A Part of You!
I Will Never Let My Love for You, Ever Vanish.
Before That Happens, I will enroll in Every University;
Until I Speak Fluent Spanish!
I Got So Much Love to Give And It's All for You.
That's Why:
I Want To Make My Love A Part of You!

My Love

The First Time I Laid Eyes on You Girl,
I knew I Would Always Remember
Your Image and Smile!
From that Day Forward;
I Programmed Your Features And
Numbers Into My Personal Brain Files.
My Love, You Are So Beautiful;
That if The Universal God Force,
Would Manifest Himself into the flesh;
He would Agree with my Assessment of what
A Fine Person You Are.
He Then Would Share Your Whole Beauty,
With Everyone Else!
I know this is a Serious Situation;
And I hope that no one have to bump heads, and
Cause More Complications.
I Prayed Long and Hard, to get help with This One.
Our Heavenly Father Revealed to me:
That I Can't Go Around Claiming This or That;
Without His Principles Remaining Intact.
Girl, I want to leave you with a Positive Thought.
I'll let the Whole Wide World Know:
"All of This Love I Have for You;
Can Never Be, Taught or Brought!"
With Blessings from Heaven Above and
Thanks for the Flowers, Water and the Baby Dove.
Without any Doubt, You Will Always Be:
My Love!

Thinking of You!

Girl, I've been
Thinking of You!
Thinking, So Hard,
I don't know what to Do.
In my dreams, I've been talking.
In my sleep, I've been walking.
I'm serious; when I say:
"If you don't act right; I might be stalking."
I'm Hoping and Praying that You are Gonna,
Make My Dreams come True.
I'm just waiting to find out;
What are You going to do?
Girl, I can't wait, til We play One on One;
With Every Thing at stake; Cause, before long;
The Baker will have both of Our Images,
On Our Wedding Cake!
It's Time that We Graduate from a Bad Situation, and
Receive a Higher Degree in An Adult Education.
That's why I no longer deal with people,
Who have Bad Reputations.
I was Thinking, while Writing this poem:
Sometimes; Life can be hard, in this Cruel World.
But, Life is Great for Me and
The Best Thing is: You Are My Girl!
Now that I'm About Finish, with this Piece;
I know what, I'm about to do.
I'm Gonna find Ya and Read it to Ya;
Because: Girl, I've been,
Thinking of You!

I Got My Girl Back!

When One is in Love with Someone;
At times, things may get off track.
All I know is, I Thank God;
I Got My Girl Back!
Although, I have the Gift to Talk;
My Girl got tired of my mouth and
Began to think I was Wack.
After all that, still:
I Got My Girl Back!
I know sometimes, I get carried away,
And at times, there is way,
Too much Yack.
This time around,
I almost went too far,
And almost got Jack!
Yet, Life is Wonderful for me; Because:
I Got My Girl Back!
My Health is Good, and I Truly Believe,
That if I start back working out; I'll be Stack!
From this Day Forward,
I'm Willing to make a Pact,
Cause:
I Got My Girl Back!
I Love this Girl;
More Than Many May Know.
It's Public Knowledge and
A Matter of Fact;
But, The Most Magnificent Thing of All Is:
I Got My Girl Back!

This Poem Has A Sweet Scent To It!

Girl, I'm sitting down, Thinking;
After You Left My View.
I Got You All Over My Mind!
People around Me are asking:
What are You writing about?
But I won't tell, So They don't have a clue.
This Poem Has A Sweet Scent To It!
After Reading It;
Only You And I Know What To Do!
Baby, You and I will have
A Fortuned and Bright Future.
I Can See Us Growing Old, While Singing,
The Greatest Hits of Luther.
Honey, I have Seen You at work and
I have Seen You at play.
Girl, I can't wait to take You on
My Granddaddy's farm,
So We Can Have A Roll In The Hay!
I Know That:
This Poem Has A Sweet Scent To It!
After Reading It;
Only You And I Know What To Do!
Though, I'm not crazy about water;
Just To Be With You,
I'll Sail in the Deepest Parts of the Oceans Blue,
While Paddling a Boat with One Shoe.
Sister, Our Love, Our Bodies and Our Spirits
Are A Perfect Fit. That's the Reason:
This Poem Has A Sweet Scent To It!

I Miss You Much!

Girl, I Miss Seeing Your Beautiful Smile.
When I'm away from You, for more than a minute;
Just to See It Again, I'll Travel a Million Miles.
When I Can't See You,
I'm Willing to Collect Every Coin On This Planet,
To Use to Call to Hear Your Lovely Voice.
I don't care what Newspaper or
Magazine Say about Us;
Even if the National Enquirer is the Source.
When We are Together,
Just to be in Your Presence,
Makes Me Feel Like the C.E.O. of AT&T.
Because; All I want to do is:
Reach Out And Touch!
That's Why, When You are not here:
Girl, I Miss You Much!
I Think About You Baby, All the Time.
I Just Can't Get You Off of My Mind!
The First Time I Laid Eyes On You,
I Must Admit, I Had A Crush!
That's why, when You are not here;
Girl, I Miss You Much!
I'm So Happy to Be Your Man and
So, Bless to Be in the Human Race.
That's why, when I'm with You,
Every Man Marvel at My Good Taste!
I Will Always Love You, from Dawn to Dusk.
That's Why, Girl, when You are not here,
I Miss You Much!

Girl, I'm So Into You!

Girl, I'm So Into You;
I Don't Know What In The World To Do.
There Were Times,
When I couldn't go to no one else.
You Gave Me So Much Love;
You Made Me Think,
You Loved Me More than I Loved Myself.
Each Day, I'm Living for the Love of You.
When You Are Around,
I Resort to Being a kid at the age of two.
Everyone knows that One have to think
Like a Child to Really Give True Love.
That's the Reason Why,
I Refuse to Give Up My Love for
This Special Beautiful Girl!
Girl, I'm So Into You;
The United States Congress
Can't Stop What We Are About To Do!
I'm So In Love With You And I Know,
There will Be A High Price To Pay.
I can't worry about that now.
I Love You as Much as a Child Loves to Play.
Now, It's My Turn to Give You Good Love!
By the Time, I'm Through With You;
Both Our Heads Will Be Spinning Around This World!
In the Body of This Poem, I have Left Everyone A Clue!
It Doesn't Matter Though; I'm Still Gonna Do,
What I Have To Do; Because:
Girl, I'm So Into You!

Girl, I Love To Hear Your Name Call

Girl, I Love To Hear Your Name Call.
When This happens; The Muscles in My Body;
Seems to Grow Ten Feet Tall!
It Happens Every Time, I'm Around You.
Seeing Those Pretty Big Brown Eyes are
The First Clue. Baby, You need to know,
Just What All of Your Finest and Beauty Do To Me.
They Make Me Feel Like Moses And
I'm About To Part The Red Sea!
I'm Ready To Give You All The Love,
That You Can Handle.
Back to Brother Moses:
"If Need Be, I'm Prepared to Walk Around
This Entire World, Wearing Leather Sandals."
Girl, You have such an Unique and Beautiful Name;
And Think About This:
"All of Our Children Will Be Full of The Spirit, And
We All Will have Fortune and Fame"
I Really Love Your Style!
Although, I haven't Exercise in Awhile.
To Hear Your Name Again and Again.
I'll Run a 26.2 Mile Marathon,
And I Guarantee You, I'll Win!
So Get Prepared To Do,
All Your Shopping at the Beverly Hills Mall!
Because; I'm Gonna Page Ya; Cause:
Girl, I Love To Hear Your Name Call.

Heavenly Sent

I Remember the First and Last Time,
That We were on the Phone;
When Our Conversation was over and We lost contact.
There was a weird Sensation in the Limbs of My Body;
That caused them to retract.
Just to think of All the Beautiful Women,
That I have Ever Known.
It's You, Who is the Inspiration for All of
My Love Poems.
Sister, You are So Sexy and So Dynamic;
You have a Glow!
You are my Best Kept Secret; But if I have to,
I'm willing to let the Whole World Know.
God has a way of turning a bad situation
Into Something Good.
I have been Searching for You, All of My Life and
Have Never Found Anyone that Compares to You,
In Any Hood! I Know that You Are:
Heavenly Sent
Because, To Get Your Love;
I'm Ready To Make Every Man Get On
His Knees To Pray And Repent!
You Are The Baddest Woman,
That Has Ever Walk On The Planet Earth.
The Reason I Say This Is: Because, Without Your Love,
My Heart Would Really Hurt.
Everyone That We Know Are Hip to My Hints.
Just Like Me, They All Know That You Are:
Heavenly Sent!

I'm Just A Fool For You

Girl, You Got Me Wishing For You.
Wishing So Hard, I Don't Know What To Do.
I'm Just A Fool For You.
Let's Do What Ever You Want To Do,
A Park, A Movie or A Bite For Two!
Tell Me What You Want To Do: I'm Just A Fool For You.
Girl, You Got Me Wishing For You.
I Admit, I'm Just A Big Fool For You;
I'll Run To You, In the Cold, Snow or Rain;
It Doesn't Matter, I'm Tired of Playing Games!
Some May Act Like it's Irrational or It's not Sane;
But, Girl You Got Me Wishing For You;
Wishing So Hard, I Don't Know What To Do.
I'm Just A Fool For You.
Let's Do What Ever You Want To Do.
I'll Pay for Our Love Light Flight To Kenya, Paris or
Any of the Islands To Get A Different View.
Tell Me What You Want To Do.
I'm Just A Fool For You.
Girl, You Got Me Wishing For You;
I've Been Thinking So Hard; I Don't Know What To Do.
I Admit, I'm Just A Big Fool For You;
I Can't Get You Off of My Mind; I'll Run To You,
Whether There Be Lighting, Thunder, Sleet or Rain;
Because, It's Only Your Love That Can Ease My Pain.
I Mean It When I Say, I'm Tired of Playing Games.
Girl, You Got Me Wishing For You;
Tell Me What You Want to Do.
I'm Just A Fool For You.

Girl, You Are So Special To Me

You have Heard the Saying:
"To Be or Not To Be"
I Like This One Better:
"Girl, You Are So Special To Me"
You are a Bright Light in My World.
You are Also the Earth's Most Pretties Girl!
I Just Love Calling Your Name; Saying it,
Makes My Irrational Thoughts, Turn Sane.
You have Helped Me Do Things,
I Never Knew that I Could Do.
Every Time I Think About Ya;
I Can Write A Poem or Two.
Girl, You Have The Most Beautiful Smile;
That I have Ever Seen.
Your Face, Your Body, Your Spirit;
All Glows With Gleam!
You Should Know That;
Your Body Is So Fine!
That It Be Kicking: Twenty-Four/Seven!
Every Man Dreams of having it.
I Cherish It Like Living In Heaven!
You May Not Know This;
But, You are the Best Thing that
Has Ever Happen in My Life.
Girl, You have Always been Real and
Have Always Treated Me Nice.
The Bible Says: The Truth Shall Make You Free.
That's Why, I'm Telling You:
Girl, You Are So Special To Me!

Ghetto Girl!

With A Ghetto Girl;
You'll have the Best Time in the World.
You don't have to buy Her, Diamonds and Pearls.
Cause, She Still Will Rock Your World!

Ain't Nothing Like Having;
A Ghetto Girl!
When it's Cloudy Outside And You are Home Alone;
All You got to do is pick up that Phone.
Dial that Number and Listen for the Tone.
Before lone, your Ghetto Girl;
Will Be On Her Way Home.

She's the Original Badd Mama Jamma!
She's a Beautiful Sight to See!
Just as Fine as She Can Be!
She's Not a Bona Fide Player; For Real.
She Just Wants To Get In Your Grill.
She Will Prepare Your First And Last Meal;
But She's Still Not A Player For Real.

I Must Admit Still;
I Too Want To Get Into Her Grill;
And Always Remain in Her World.
Cause, With All My Love;
She Will Always Be,
My Ghetto,
Ghetto Girl!

I Ain't Gon't Tell Nobody!

Girl; We Can Have A Show!
It's My Goal To Be With You, And
I Ain't Gon't Tell Nobody!
No One Needs To Know.
I'll say yes and still won't tell nobody;
Not even myself, If it would help,
You and Me to get Unwind and to get Undress.
My Only Goal Is To Be With You.
Even to You, I won't tell it Back.
Cause, I Ain't Just Any Black!
Most of the Time, I'm Like Ciara: I'm Goodie, Goodie!
But Now, I'm Like Master P: Ugh, I'm Bout it, Bout it!
Agh; Girl, I just want You to, Ugh;
Make me Holla, Holla; Agh!
Because, I Feel You Are Mine, and
I Oughta, Oughta, Get it, Get it!
Tell Me That You Are That Somebody; That,
I Ain't Gon't Tell Nobody; Bout it, Bout it!
That You Are Gonna Make Me; Holla, Holla!
When I Get Some of That; Goodie, Goodie!
Even to You, I won't tell it Back.
Cause, I Ain't Just Any Black!
I'll say yes and still won't tell nobody;
Not even myself; If it would help;
You and Me, To get Unwind and to get Undress.
Girl; We Can Have A Show!
It's My Goal To Be With You, And
I Ain't Gon't Tell Nobody!
No One Needs To Know.

All I Want You To Do,
Is To Give Me A Little Bit of You!

I Watch You Time After Time, Walk By Me.
I Must Admit, In the Past, I Didn't Know What To Say.
I'm Not the Only One. Every Other Man I Observed;
Responds In the Same Way.
I'm Hoping You Are Gonna Do
What I Want You To Do And
Give Me A Little Bit of You!
I've Been Praying So Hard,
I Don't Know What In The World To Do.
I May Not Be Using The Right Words To Say;
Because The Words May Be Getting In The Way.
All I Know Is, I Want To Be With You.
I've Been Watching The Wonderful Things You Do.
All I Want You To Do,
Is To Give Me A Little Bit of You!
I've Been Observing You For So Long.
Honey, You Are Always On My Mind.
Girl, You Got Me Staying Up All Night;
Hearing My Old LP's of Prince, Vanity And The Time!
Baby, The Whole World Admires Your Beauty And
Loves The Beautiful Things You Do.
I May Not Be Using The Right Words To Say;
Because The Words May Be Getting In The Way.
All I Know Is, I Want To Be With You.
I've Been Watching The Wonderful Things You Do.
All I Want You To Do,
Is To Give Me A Little Bit of You!

I'm Trapped Inside Your Love

Baby, I'm Trapped Inside Your Love,
And it's no mistake; Because,
You are The Chocolate Icing On My Cake!
It All Happen the First Time I Laid Eyes On You.
I Knew It Would Occur,
There was nothing I could do.
My Love for You; Flows from my beginning to
The Heavenly Fathers Never Ending
My Love is Deeper than Any Ocean And
I'm Not Pretending.
I'm Saturated in You And There's No Escape.
There's a Beautiful Life in store for Us and I can't wait.
I Thought I Knew The True Meaning of Real Love.
Honey; Let Me Tell You Something:
The Caring and Feelins That You Have Shown Me;
Can Be A Lesson for All Boys and Girls!
Baby, You Have Turned On
A Light and Have Rejuvenated a Pulse,
In My Heart That No Other Woman Have Had
The Tools or Desire to Bestow to Such
An Electric Source from Dawn to Dusk.
We're Trapped Inside This Love And
There's No Mistake.
I Want You to Know That We Have Reached A Point,
Where There Is No Escape.
Without Your Love; We Have Nothing.
Therefore: I Surrender with Blessings from
The Father from Heaven Above! Because:
I'm Trapped Inside Your Love!

Girl, I'm Stone In Love With You

Don't Stop My Love for You, Whatever You Do.
Cause: Girl, I'm Stone In Love With You.
Here's the Key to My Heart And
Only You Can Unlock It.
Baby, When It Comes to My Love;
Please Tell Me That You'll Never Stop It.
In the past, I use to hold My Love back;
Not any more, now I come Faster than a
Greasy Man's Heart Attack!
Don't Stop My Love for You, Whatever You Do.
Cause: Girl, I'm Stone In Love With You.
There shouldn't be any doubt in Your Mind that
Our Love Won't Last.
Please, Don't Judge Me On What Bums did in the past.
Girl, the way I see it, we got more to Gain than to lose.
Just think, Out of All The Women In The World;
You Are The One I Choose!
Don't Stop My Love for You, Whatever You Do.
Cause: Girl, I'm Stone In Love With You.
There's Not A Soul On This Planet,
Who Can Stop My Love for You!
So, Baby; I Wanna Know:
What Are You Gonna Do?
Every Minute That I'm Awake,
I'm Thinking About You!
So, Baby; I Wanna Know:
What Are You Gonna Do?
Don't Stop My Love for You, Whatever You Do.
Cause: Girl, I'm Stone In Love With You!

I Got A Brand New High!

The Way You Make Me Feel Is So Special.
It's A Love That No One Can Buy.
That's Why, When You Came on the Scene;
I Got A Brand New High!
Thinking About You Really makes Me Excited.
Every One can tell, because Sparks comes from
My Heart, Which is Brightly Lighted.
When You Are In My Presence,
My Whole Body Has Da Rise!
Because It Knows Before Long,
That It Will have the Grand Prize.
You have So Much Beauty and Charm;
To Keep the World's Population Asleep; And
To Continue to Be Around You,
I will Repeatedly Hit the Buttons:
On Anyone's Clock Alarm!
When I First Saw Your Image On
That Bright Sunny Day;
Your Inner and Outer Beauty Showed Me
A Brand New Way!
I Once Thought I Knew What True Love Was.
Now I Realize,
You Are The Only Real Woman for Me.
Those others were just girls.
It's So Good To Know That We Will Never Ever,
Have to Say Bye, Bye;
Because,   I Thank God:
I Got A Brand New High!

Help Yourself To Another Serving of My Love

Girl, Before I Saw Ya;
I Met You in My Dreams.
You Are Love!
And is the One, Who Makes Me Sing.
Tell All Perpetrators that
They Better Get Back! And
That They Can't Have Any of This Helping;
Not Even A Midnight Snack!
Many Have Seen Me in Action and
They Know; I Don't Play!
When it Comes to You.
My Player Days Are Long Gone and
I Sang These Songs on Que!
Some have even said that I may have lost my mind.
Those are only rumors, because as long as,
God and You Loves Me,
I Will Always Know The Time!
Life is Wonderful, Since I Received Your Love.
Ooh! The Way You Give It!
Makes Me, Higher Than The Clouds Above!
Girl, You Are A Star In My Eyes!
You know I've Always Been Honest and
I Don't Tell Lies.
Baby, It's Time That You Get off Work and
Remove Your Gloves.
Hurry Home and Open the Door To Our World. And:
Help Yourself To Another Serving of My Love!

What To Do With All This Love

When People in this World treats me in a bad way;
This Beautiful Black Sister seems to be The Only One,
Who Can Calm Me Down Without Delay.
Shakespeare wrote about Romantic Love,
That's Eros!
I Feel That Love Coming from the Both of Us,
So Get Ready to Toast!
We Have A Friendship That Will Never End,
That's Phileo!
Let's Let The Whole Wide World Know.
We Have Been Committed to This Love from the Start.
So On the Mark, Get Ready, Get Set, Go!
I Know That It's God's Love Within You;
That's Agape'
That is Doing All of These Beautiful Things,
That's Why For You, Girl:
"I Can't Wait to Buy You that Ring"
To Show Our True Love And Our Strong Bond:
On Our Wedding Day, Let's Get Prepared to Sang
Our Favorite Temptations Song!
I Know Now, What it's Like to Be in Heaven.
Because With God's Blessing, I Think About This Sister
Twenty-Four/Seven! In the Body of this Piece,
I have Mentioned some of the Major Kinds of Love;
Which are Within This World.
I'm So Happy and Grateful, God Allowed Me to Know
This Fine Black Girl!
That's The Reason Why, I Don't Know,
What To Do With All This Love!

Vision of You!

I Think About You Baby, All the Time.
I Wake Up Every Morning
With Your Image On My Mind.
I have to Watch the Movement of My Steps;
Because, When I have This Vision:
"My Heart Really Needs Some Help"
I'm Hoping that We will be Together in Due Time,
So That My Heart Doesn't Fall Out of
This Body of Mine.
I Can See You at this Given Moment;
With Your Brown Skin like the Sand;
And Your Tender Lips as Soft as the Shore.
They Leave Me Wanting You More and More!
I Don't Know What We Are Going to Do,
When We are Finally Alone and Together.
Right Now I Can Visualize Seeing
Stars and Being in Heaven!
What I Like about You the Most Is,
You are not Aware of How Fine and Beautiful You Are!
If I was a kid again:
"You Would Be the Only Present that
I Would Un-Wrap As My Christmas Toy!"
Each Night I Pray to The Father and ask Him:
What Should I Do?
I Must Be Doing Something Right!
Because, He Still Allows Me;
To Have A
Vision of You!

Shadow Love

All of This Time,
I Thought I Stole Your Heart And
Won A Major Battle.
But in Reality, When I Was With You;
I Was Making Love to Your Shadow.
When I Was Screaming Your Name,
Early in the Morning and Late at Night; I Must Admit,
Making Love to Your Shadow, Felt Alright.
Sometimes, Shadow Loving is O.K.
But, I Want to Try Something New, That Feels Alright,
Hold My Pillow Tight and Fall Asleep,
With Someone as Beautiful as You And
Never Be Alone Again at Night.
I Know That You Like a Nice Looking Man,
With a Pleasant Voice,
Who at Times Can Sound a little,
Like Marvin, When He Sang.
I Like a Woman with Similar Characteristics;
That's Why, When I Think of You,
I Listen to My Whitney CD's And Grab a Coke;
Because, I Like the Real Thang!
Now That I have Awaken from
This Unbelievable Dream,
That has come to an End.
Hit Me Up On The Phone,
Then Come Over and I Promise,
We Will Never Have to Make
Shadow Love
And Never Ever Be Alone Again!

Love Poems

Today is Our Day. All I Got to Say;
It Seems Like We Have Known
One Another Before We Were Born.
Girl, That's One of the Reasons, Why
I'm Writing You These
Love Poems.
I Appreciate You for Being My Friend.
If I Can Be of Any Assistance to You;
I Want You to Know, I'll be helpful til the End.
You Are So Beautiful; Inside and Out! Therefore:
"You Will Always Be Special to Me, Without A Doubt"
It's So Amazing That God Allowed Us
To Be Friends and to Remain True.
That's Another Reason, Why
I Have So Much Love for You!
You Have So Much Beauty and You're So Fine.
Baby, That's Why I Know;
You Are One of A Kind!
There Are Many Times I Feel
That You Are All I Got.
I Want The World To Know:
"You Are The One I Love
And Is The One Who Keeps Me Hot!"
If You Were Here, I Would Sang You
A Couple of Our Favorite Songs!
But, I'm Gonna Try And Do A Little Better, and
When I See You, I'm Gonna Give You
A Signed Copy of Our,
Love Poems!

Our Love

There's No Doubt That Our Love is Real.
Right now, I Don't Care, Who Knows How I Feel.
Our Love is Greater Than the Number of fish in the sea.
Our Love Will Multiply More Than
The Mother of the Most Powerful queen bee.
Our Love is Smoother Than
The Most Pleasant Gentle Breeze.
Our Love Has Me Groaning Like
James Brown: Please Please Please!
I Must Admit, Your Love Took Me By Surprise!
From This Moment Forward;
Your Beauty Will Never Leave My Eyes.
If We Are Ever Separated; I Will Search for You,
Behind Every Door And
Then I'll Beg for Your Love, More And More.
To Calm My Storm; All You have to Do is Give Me,
My Most Favorite Chocolate Treat;
For That Alone, If Need Be,
I'm Prepared to Rub Your Aching Feet.
I have Waited All My Life to Discover You!
There's No Way, I'm Backing Down Now;
No Matter What Obstacles Are Directed Our Way.
Once We Begin the Process of Living Our Life,
Together as One, Daily We'll Get on Our Knees to Pray.
I Want the World to Know, I'm Never Gonna Let You Go!
Just to Think:
I Have The Most Beautiful Girl In The Whole World!
Our Flame Will Burn, Forever and Ever, To Show:
Our Love!

That's A Fine, That's A Fine, That's A Fine, Girl!

Every Time I see Ya,
Even without Touching,
You Still Rocks My World!
Whether You Wear Your Hair:
Straight, Nappy or in Curls;
Sister; Your Glow is More Beautiful
Than Any Diamond or Pearl!
That's A Fine, That's A Fine, That's A Fine, Girl!

When I See your Walk;
You Throw Them Hips from Left to Right!
Your Movement is More Powerful;
Than a Venus or Serena Serve!!
That's A Fine, That's A Fine, That's A Fine, Girl!

Baby, Although You often wear loose fitting Clothing;
That Would Cover Up the Assets of Most Fine Girls.
When You wear Similar Clothes,
Your Figure Is Still Revealed And Looks
Fresher than a New Born Baby Dove!
That's A Fine, That's A Fine, That's A Fine, Girl!

Honey, You're Finer Than The Baddest Majorette,
Marching With A Baton That Twirls.
I'm So Bless To Be In Your World:
That's A Fine, That's A Fine, That's A Fine, Girl!

He'll Never Love You Like I Do

He can't touch you! He can't hug you!
He can't hold you! He'll never Love you like I do!
Just because he brought you that diamond;
And one time gave you a string of pearls.
He also brags to his boys that he rocks your world.
He can't touch you! He can't hug you!
He can't hold you! He'll never Love you like I do!
He claims that he is a big time star; And says
The reason he's never home is because
He has been on The road most nights;
And he tells everyone that he gives you good Love.
He can't touch you! He can't hug you!
He can't hold you! He'll never Love you like I do!
So you think your mind is made up; And
He has convinced you to close the door.
Now you worship the ground he walks on And
Thinks he's everything; But, when it comes to Love,
I Can Give You More.
He can't touch you! He can't hug you!
He can't hold you! He'll never Love you like I do!
He may give you diamond rings, pearls and Lots of
Pretty things; But, It's my Heart that makes you Sing!
One Thang for Sho', you know that I Love you,
And he's not capable of Loving you like I do.
Not only do I give Good Love; But; My Love is
Saturated with Love from Heavenly Places from Above!
He can't Touch You! He can't Hug You!
He can't Hold You!
He'll Never Love You Like I Do!

Only Yesterday

My First Time Laying Eyes on this
Black Beautiful Sister was Only Yesterday!
Any Decent Man Who Were in My Shoes
At That Given Moment, Would have Gotten on
His Knees, Without Delay, To Pray and Give Thanks to Our
Heavenly Father and Ask Him for Strength, Wisdom and
Direction, for Such A Beautiful, Charming and Pleasant
Smelling Scent That Flows From This Body, Soul and Spirit of
The Woman of Any Good Man's Dream.
From the First Time We Laid Eyes On One Another;
I knew, Right then, that I had known Her, All of My Life.
She was that skinny little Brown Girl I wanted to
Give My First Kiss to and found a Ring and gave to Her.
But Members from Both of Our Families, objected to it.
She was the First Girl I asked for Her phone number;
But we never could Get Connected.
After All of those years; She still has The Flavor and
The Dimensions that I Desire in a Lady.
She's not Too Tall, She's not too short, She's not Fat,
She's no longer skinny; She's Stack, Just Right!
The Reason I know, She's the One! Because,
She has Always had my Back in Every Right Situation!
She has Never tried to Belittle Me or has
Never tried to Embarrass One to get a Cheap Laugh.
I Know She's Been Mines, Before Time;
By the Revealing of The Spirit; From Our Holy Father!
When The Lighting Flash; You Will See!
I Believe This is a Good Thang!
The Way God Revealed to Joseph, About Mary in a Dream;
He Revealed Something to Me, in a Similar Way.
The Only Difference is He Spoke to Me About Her
Only Yesterday!

If You Help Me With The Loving, I'll Do All The Kissing!

Girl, If You Help Me With The Loving,
I'll Do All The Kissing!
I'm Gonna Make You Say:
Stop! "Oh" Don't Stop! Stop! "Oh" Don't Stop!
If You Help Me With The Loving, I'll Do All The Kissing!
I'll Kiss You Right!
Some may say, I'll Kiss You Wrong!
I'll Do All The Kissing All Night Long!
Honey, If You Help Me With The Loving,
I'll Do All The Kissing!
I'll Kiss You When The Sun Is Up!
I'll Kiss you when it's down!
I'll Kiss You When The Stars are Bright!
I'll Kiss You when they seem to have no light!
Baby Can't You See, This Could Take All Night!
If You Help Me With The Loving, I'll Do All The Kissing!
After All We been Through, I keep Coming Back to You.
I don't care how Many Women wear
Diamonds and Pearls.
Between The Two of Us, I'll Do All The Kissing!
Because, You Are Out of This World!
But The Most Important Thing of All Is:
You Are My Girl!
There's No Time for A Whole Lot of Wishing; Because,
If You Help Me With The Loving,
I'll Do All The Kissing!

I Don't Want Any Love!
I Want Your Love!

Every One Needs Love, That's No Doubt.
My Love is Gonna Get Ya in Areas
Which have Never Been Sought!
I'm Laying Every Thing On the Table
And is Willing and Able to Fight
Any Battle That Needs to Be Fought!,
You Better Believe That My Love is
Gonna Get Ya, That's No Doubt!
I Don't Want Any Love! I Want Your Love!
Love Won't Let Me Wait, Another Day.
I Don't Want Any Love! I Want Your Love!
Love Won't Let Me Wait, Another Hour.
I Don't Want Any Love! I Want Your Love!
Love Won't Let Me Wait, Another Minute.
I Don't Want Any Love! I Want Your Love!
Love Won't Let Me Wait, Another Second.
I Don't Want Any Love! I Want Your Love!
Only You And I Can Experience This Ecstasy.
After We Touch, There Will Be An Explosion!
By the Time We Are Through, The Aftermath
Will Look Like The Hardest Worker Bees,
Best Production; Ever Presented
To The Most Powerful African Queen Bee!
And The Finest Drippings from
Any Maple or Honey Tree!
I Just Can't Wait, Love Won't Let Me Wait.
I Don't Want Any Love! I Want Your Love!

Baby, Your Kiss Gave Me Life!

Someone in Heaven Led Me to You.
The Whole Earth Shook And Felt My Heart Beat Too!
If I Ever Lose You, I Will Keep Trying to Find You.
I Cried and Made the Ultimate Sacrifice; Because:
Baby, Your Kiss Gave Me Life!
You Must Be An Angel in Disguise;
Because, When You Are Not Here;
The Only Thing That Calms Me Down,
Is When You Reappear And Is Back By My Side.
I asked our Heavenly Father, to send me Someone to Love.
As the Thunder Roared And as the Lighting Flashed!
You Soon Appeared to Me, And
I Knew That You Were Sent From Heaven Above!
To Keep Getting Love From You, Again And Again;
I'm Willing to Pay The Ultimate Price; Because:
Baby, Your Kiss Gave Me Life!
I Know We Are In An Unique Situation; But, That's All Right,
Cause I'm Willing to Ride This Boat;
Until We Have No More Complications.
Girl, I Know We Have Cut Off A Big Slice;
But, I Can't Help Myself; Because:
Baby, Your Kiss Gave Me Life!
Since, We First Met; You Have Always Been Real And Has
Always Treated Me Nice. I Don't Know What All Was In It, But:
Baby, Your Kiss Gave Me Life!
As Stated Before, Someone In Heaven Led Me to You.
I Am So Happy And Grateful That It Happen;
If Not, I Don't Know What in the World, I Would Do.
We All Know Who It Was:
Our Savior, Our Lord, Our King, Our Christ!
Girl, He allowed you to Touch Me, and:
Baby, Your Kiss Gave Me Life!

My Nubian Queen!

I Know This Fine Girl.
Every Time I See This Woman;
She Dresses Impeccable And Is Always Clean.
I have Observed Individuals mistreat Her.
She Never Returns the Favor, By treating them mean.
I Thank God Every Day for the Sun, the Stars and
Bringing Her into My Life; Because, She's
My Nubian Queen!
There are Moments When People think that I'm
Trying to be funny or that I may be wasting their time.
That's not it at all; What the Deal is:
I Got This Beautiful Sister, All Over My Mind!
Every Second That I'm Away from Her;
You Just Don't Know; How Much My Heart Suffers.
If You don't believe Me; The next time it happens;
Hook It Up to an EKG Machine; I Guarantee Ya,
It'll Sound Like a Car Without a Muffler.
In the Past; I Use to Dream That the Day Would Come
And She Would Be All Mine.
Mark My Word: There Will Come the Day When Me and
This Sister Will have the Cure to Heal the World.
Just for that reason alone; One should understand:
Why I have So Much Love for,
That Fine Girl!
So the Next Time, You Greet Me and
You think that I'm being mean, that's not it at all.
I'm Just Preparing a Path; For:
My Nubian Queen!

I Love You, Because You Love Me

Girl, It's hard to believe that within a year;
I have Written A Whole Book About You!
Usher and Alicia may play the Right Keys;
But it's You, Who is My Boo!
I know that I have known You; Before We came to Be.
You have helped Me, to Open My Eyes.
I once was blind, but Now I Can Clearly See!
I Love You, Because You Love Me.
Girl, I Put My Trust in You, So What Ever You Do;
Don't Take Your Love Away from Me.
I Love You, Because You Love Me.
Your Love has Shown Me the Right Way.
I Don't Care What Others Might Say.
It's Your Smile That Brightens My Day.
That's The Reason, I Will Never Go Away.
When I'm With You; I Can't Imagine, Any Place Being
Any Better; To Stay Near And Close To You;
I'm Willing To Delay My Date In Going To Heaven!
When I'm Away from You for
More Than A Day or Two;
Then You Reappear And Your Face, Body And Spirit,
Looks Brander Than New!
Girl, When You Came On The Scene;
You Were More Than Just Good Luck!
I Don't Know if It's Possible, but Baby,
I Think I Love You, Much than Much!
I have Unlocked My Heart And You Now have the Key.
I Want You To Always Remember This:
I Love You, Because You Love Me!

A Beautiful Sister Day In Mint

Out of All the Days, in the World;
This is A Special Day, And
The Finest hour, for A Beautiful Girl!
Every Man That Knows You,
Would gladly volunteer to pay Your rent;
For A Chance to Be in Your Presence;
To Admire and Look at A Lady In Mint.
Everybody Loves and Cherish You on the Job.
After Meeting You, They All Say: This Work Isn't Hard.
Girl, You Are So Sweet and So Kind; You Look
So Young and Fine, You must have missed
The aging Process by Father Time.
God Brought you forth and Remembers that Day Too.
Girl, I Got Something to Tell Ya:
They Don't Come, No Finer Than You!
Before Every Dollar in This Nation's Economy is Spent;
Us Brothers and Sisters, Should Organize,
A March on Washington,
To Make A Legal Holiday, Celebrating:
A Beautiful Sister Day In Mint!
People from Around the World Will Send in
Their Last Dollars, Last Coins and Their Last Red Cent;
Just to buy Commemorative Coins and Stamps, for
A Beautiful Sister Day In Mint!
So, We will All Travel Thousands of Miles And
By Proclamation, We Will Always Remember This Day
In Our Personal Brain Files; Therefore:
I'm Asking Everyone To Get All Prayed Up And Repent.
Because, This Day Will Always Be Reserved for,
A Beautiful Sister Day In Mint!

Fly Beauty!

When I First Saw This Fine,
Fly Beauty!
I Must Admit,
I didn't know what to do.
Her Essence, Her Style and Unique Walk;
Reminded Me of My First Love,
Erykah Badu!
I Later Saw Her wearing a Headdress;
That Also Reminded Me of My Special Friend.
The Way She Smiled At Me, Was A Sign That
We Would Be Friends til the End!
She Gives Love That Is So Innocent And So Sincere.
It has the Main Ingredient of The Fathers Love,
Which is from Heaven Above, And
A Flavor of Ghetto Fabulous That
Draws Many Hearts Near.
Every One That Knows Her Is Aware That:
Beauty is Black! And Black is Beauty!
I Tell You The Truth!
Every Time, I'm In Her Presence,
She Walks And Glides In A Motion,
That Would Make Any Man,
Thankful and Grateful,
To Give Her All of His Love, And
To Perform All of His Civic And Holy Duties.
I Want To Thank You Girl for Being There for Me, and
We Will Always Be Down for
One Another And You Will Always Be My:
Fly Beauty!

Lord, Thanks For Sending Me Out An Angel

I Want to Thank You Father,
For Sending Me Out An Angel.
Like Always, You Went All The Way
And Sent One Who Loves Me In Return.
Lord, You Treat Me So Good,
I Truly Believe, I'm Your Most Favorite Son!
I Was Once Told: It Doesn't Matter,
What's The Situation or How Bad The Weather;
That Your Love Will Always Make It Better.
Lord, Thanks For Sending Me Out An Angel!
When I Woke Up!
And First Got A Glance of
That Fine Girl!
That You Sent To Me; I Must Tell Ya,
She's Been Sweeter Than Any Rice Krispies Treats.
She's That Ole Fashion Girl
That I Had A Vision of In My Sleep.
The Day Before You Introduced Her To Me,
I Had A Feelin' You Were About To Do Something Great!
That's The Reason, I Iron And
Set My Clothes Out The Night Before;
So I Would Not Be Late.
Father, Thanks For Sending Me Someone
Who is So Fine, So Smart And So Beautiful!
Thanks Also for Sending Her to Me Before We Grew Old.
As Bob Marley Once Sung: "In This Sweet Life"
Thanks for Sending Her Out to Me, Because:
"We All Are Coming In From The Cold!"
Lord, Thanks For Sending Me Out An Angel!

This Is The Day!

This Is The Day That Our Lord Has Approved!
My Player Days Are Long Gone.
Can You Believe?
I Once Thought That It Was Cool.
I'm So Glad We Met And
That We Both Went To School.
Aren't You Elated That We Made It,
Without Breaking Any Major Rules?
We Went To Christ And Found The Truth.
He Now Lives In Me And You.
It feels so Good to Testify, when most don't have a clue.
I Cherish Each Day That I Spend With You.
This Is The Day That Our Lord Has Approved!
Here's the Ring: Which will Act as the Bond with Glue.
Honey I'm On One Knee, Baby Please Say I Do.
When We are Married, We'll have a Child or Two.
No Matter what ever happens, you'll always be my Boo!
I Just can't stand the time when I'm away from You.
You Are So Beautiful! What's A Man Suppose To Do?
I Want to Thank You for Saying Yes And
For Agreeing to Always Be True!
At this given Moment, I want to Feel Me Inside of You;
But, I know We will have to wait Until June, one two!
I Want You to Know That I Will Never
Jeopardize or Damage My Relationship with You.
Our Spirits, Our Souls And Our Bodies
Will Remain As One With Our Heavenly Father,
Even After The Earth and The Heavens Are Made New.
This Is The Day That Our Lord Has Approved!

"My Beautiful Black Sisters"

Oh! You All are the Spice of Life!
Without You; There would never be the possibility of Me.
Every Man can walk around with His chest out;
But He plus any other being;
Could have produced anything, Without
My Beautiful Black Sisters!
People in the media, can talk about The Black
Broken Family, All Day Long; But from Big Mama Nem,
To the Young Sisters in the Hood Today.
They have Always been the Ones, Who Gave Us True Love.
Let me tell Y'all Sisters something: You All are A Wonder!
In The Beginning; The Creator Revealed to The Universe,
That: My Beautiful Black Sisters
Are The Key to Life!
You were the First Ones
To Raise the Children in The Village.
You Were The First Teachers.
You All are Better than any Religion made by Man.
It was You, Who introduced Us to Our Heavenly Father!
Through Him; you showed us how to Live a Holy Life.
Just to be in Your Presence; Makes My Body Quiver,
And tears are flowing from My Face,
While writing the rough draft of this poem.
When the Light Shines on You;
My Beautiful Black Sisters;
Even Your Shadow has A Glow!
If All of You would disappear from the Planet Today,
All Life form left behind;
Wouldn't last a second without You.
"My Beautiful Black Sisters"

Acknowledgments from Barry Thomas

I Give the Up Most Respect and Thanks to the Reverend Jesse Jackson,
For Allowing Me to be a Delegate and for Allowing Me to Work in
His 1988 Presidential Campaign. Sir, You and Your Team
Taught and Showed Me How the Political System Work.

I Love You Brother!

Thanks to Tom Joyner, Bill Cosby, Michael Jordan and William Gray.

I Give Thanks with Gratitude to My Mother, My Granddaddy,
Brothers, Sisters, Uncles, Aunts, Nieces, Nephews, Cousins,
Teachers, Students, Supporters and All My Friends.

I Love You, Dearly!

Thanks to All "My Beautiful Black Sisters"
Who Gave and Continue to Give Me Much Much Love.

You All Are: That Fine Girls!!!!   I Love You All!

Finally, I Would Like to Praise the Most Important One in my life.
Our Holy Father, Jesus Christ.

Because, He is Truly Amazing!

Amazing

Jesus Christ
Is So Amazing;
That the word Amazing;
Is not an Amazing enough
of a word to describe
How Amazing,
He Truly Is!

Jesus Christ
Is So Awesome;
That His Awesomeness,
Is an Awesomeness
That man can not
Comprehend!

Jesus Christ
Is So Good,
That His Goodness
Is in His Power!
In His Everlasting!
In His Mercy!
In His Never Ending!
And
Most Importantly,
By His Grace!

Faith

We have read His Word; It States That:
Now Faith is the Substance of Things Hoped for,
The Evidence of Things not seen.
Do you really know, what that means?
By Gods Word: "He Created The Whole World"
The Things that we see, were not made
By man, woman, a boy or a girl.
These Things were made by Things,
Which do not appear by the Naked Eye.
Noah was warned by God of things,
Not yet seen and His Family was Saved;
But the rest of the World was lost,
And it was too late to Cry.
Without Faith it is Impossible to please God.
The First Step is to come to Him and to Be Real.
You then Must Believe in Him and Believe That
He is a Rewarder of Those Who Seeks Him,
And that He is The Cure for All ills!
Faith is like, Allowing God to be your Spokesman
And before any Action or Anything comes out of
Your Body or Mouth, It has to be Cleared by God.
So, Before you Speak, Walk, Eat or Do Anything;
Get Clearance from The Father.
Now that Doesn't Seem So Hard;
When You are Really and Truly
Riding With God!

The Author

Barry Thomas was Born in Mobile Alabama.
He is a Graduate of Murphy High School.
Mr. Thomas Received a Bachelor of Science Degree in
Electrical Engineering from Tuskegee University.

This is Barry Thomas First Book Published.